COUNTRYSIDE A BIRDS OF NEW ZEALAND

This new book has a specific purpose — namely, to help bird watchers identify the birds most commonly seen in suburban gardens, city parks, domains and reserves, or farms and orchards. With this object, varying stages in growth are illustrated, as well as seasonal changes in plumage, and birds which can be confusing are grouped together. A further advantage of this work is the greater size of the painted specimens, compared with those commonly shown in bird guides.

The text is deliberately concise, consisting mainly of features that cannot be easily illustrated, and some useful facts about relationships — species, genus, family.

Books by Elaine Power

Small Birds of the New Zealand Bush (Collins)
Waders in New Zealand (Collins)
New Zealand Water Birds (Collins)
Seabirds of New Zealand (Collins)
Elaine Power's Living Garden (Hodder)

Books illustrated by Elaine Power

Tat, by Neil McNaughton (Collins)
The Horse in New Zealand, by Len McClelland (Collins)
Wild Manes in the Afternoon, by Mary Cox (Collins)
The New Guide to the Birds of New Zealand, by Falla *et al.* (Collins)
The Herb Garden Displayed, by Gillian Painter (Hodder)
A Touch of Nature, by Muriel Fisher (Collins)
Old Fashioned and Unusual Herbs, by Gillian Painter (Hodder)
Our Trees, by Frank Newhook (Bateman)
Call of the Kotuku, by Janet Redhead (Hodder)
The Pohutukawa Tree, by Ron Bacon (School Pubs.)

COUNTRYSIDE AND GARDEN BIRDS OF NEW ZEALAND

Elaine Power

DAVID BATEMAN
AUCKLAND

About the Artist

Elaine Power was born in Auckland in 1931, educated at Diocesan High School for Girls in Auckland and spent a year at the Elam School of Fine Arts. Was a librarian at the Remuera Library for five years. After a year as a doctor's receptionist spent the years before marriage, with the mapping department of the Automobile Association. Married Gerald Aldworth Power. When their third daughter was three, started painting again and submitted designs to the Crown Lynn Pottery Design competition. Highly commended. Submitted first paintings of birds to William Collins in 1968 and her first book was commissioned.

© Elaine Power 1987

First published in 1987
by David Bateman Ltd.,
'Golden Heights', 32-34 View Road, Glenfield,
Auckland, New Zealand

Typeset by Typocrafters Ltd
Printed by Colorcraft Ltd, Hong Kong

ISBN 0-908610-76-9

All rights reserved. No part of this publication may be reproduced or transmitted in any form or by any means, without permission.

Contents

	page
Pheasant: *Phasianus colchicus*: Family PHASIANIDAE	9–10
California quail: *Lophortyx californicus*: Family PHASIANIDAE	11–12
Brown quail: *Synoicus ypsilophorus*: Family PHASIANIDAE	11–12
House sparrow: *Passer domesticus*: Family PLOCEIDAE	13–14
Hedge sparrow: *Prunella modularis*: Family PRUNELLIDAE	13–14
Fantail: *Rhipidura fuliginosa*: Family MUSCICAPIDAE	15–16
Grey warbler: *Gerygone igata*: Family SYLVIIDAE	15–16
Shining cuckoo: *Chalcites lucidus*: Family CUCULIDAE	15–16
Silvereye: *Zosterops lateralis*: Family ZOSTEROPIDAE	17–18
Tui: *Prosthemadera novaeseelandiae*: Family MELIPHAGIDAE	19–20
Pukeko: *Porphyrio melanotus*: Family RALLIDAE	21–22
Cattle egret: *Bubulcus ibis*: Family ARDEIDAE	23–24
Spur-winged plover: *Lobibyx novaehollandiae*: Family CHARADRIIDAE	23–24
Welcome swallow: *Hirundo neoxena*: Family HIRUNDINIDAE	25–26
Eastern rosella: *Platycercus eximius*: Family PSITTACIDAE	27–28
New Zealand kingfisher: *Halcyon sancta*: Family ALCEDINIDAE	29–30
Harrier: *Circus approximans*: Family ACCIPITRIDAE	31–32
Little owl: *Athene noctua*: Family STRIGIDAE	31–32
Starling: *Sturnus vulgaris*: Family STURNIDAE	33–34
Myna: *Acridotheres tristis*: Family STURNIDAE	35–36
Song thrush: *Turdus philomelos*: Family TURDIDAE	35–37–38
Blackbird: *Turdus merula*: Family TURDIDAE	35–37–38
Yellowhammer: *Emberiza citrinella*: Family EMBERIZIDAE	39–40
Cirl bunting: *Emberiza cirlus*: Family EMBERIZIDAE	39–40
Chaffinch: *Fringilla coelebs*: Family FRINGILLIDAE	41–42
Greenfinch: *Carduelis chloris*: Family FRINGILLIDAE	41–42
Redpoll: *Carduelis flammea*: Family FRINGILLIDAE	43–44
Goldfinch: *Carduelis carduelis*: Family FRINGILLIDAE	43–44
Skylark: *Alauda arvensis*: Family ALAUDIDAE	45–46
New Zealand pipit: *Anthus novaeseelandiae*: Family MOTACILLIDAE	45–46
White-backed magpie: *Gymnorhina hypoleuca*: Family CRACTICIDAE	47–48
Black-backed magpie: *Gymnorhina tibicen*: Family CRACTICIDAE	47–48
Rook: *Corvus frugilegus*: Family CORVIDAE	47–48

Foreword

Elaine Power's paintings of birds and plants have made hers a household name throughout New Zealand. Of the three hundred or so birds which may be found within the limits of our long and mountainous archipelago, from the great albatrosses to the tiny riflemen, there are few which she has not sketched. Her work in the field and out at sea has been followed by a painstaking examination of specimens held in museums.

In this volume, the first of a series, the artist presents familiar birds of our gardens, farmlands and suburban parks. Overseas visitors are sometimes inclined to ask, 'Where are the native birds?' to which the answer must be 'Most are still there; but with few exceptions such as fantail, grey warbler, kingfisher, tui, they must be sought in the indigenous forests or in remote places or on offshore islands'. Most of the common species which immediately catch the eye or ear, are from Europe, especially Britain, Australia, America or the Indian region. Also in recent centuries some Australian species have flown the Tasman and settled and bred in New Zealand. Silvereye, welcome swallow, white-faced heron, spur-winged plover, coot, royal spoonbill, black-fronted dotterel, and others are now gladly accepted as genuine New Zealanders.

An avian league of nations now enlivens our countryside. Thrushes, blackbirds and skylarks are notable songsters and there is real music in the notes of chaffinches, goldfinches and Australian magpies. Yellowhammers have beautiful plumage, the males being especially delightful to look at. Mallard, black swans from Australia, pheasants from Asia, California quail are esteemed and eye-catching game birds. The range of size, shape, colour, voice and behaviour is immense.

Because of its oceanic remoteness, New Zealand lacks the great variety of land birds such as inhabit Australia or other vast continents. It is sometimes remarked that the wealth and glory of New Zealand's birds are best seen along the coast or over our coastal waters. These birds will be the subject of later volumes. So too will the distinctive endemic birds whose habitat has been so much changed by milling, agriculture and the introduction of four-legged predators.

I am sure Elaine Power's artistry will give much pleasure. These charmingly elegant little books should stimulate among their readers a desire to go out and see for themselves. They should also encourage a caring and responsible attitude towards the wonderful world of Nature.

R. B. Sibson

Introduction

Arriving in a country partly covered in dense bush, the early settlers were surprised to find only a few species of land birds and few familiar plants, so they set out to make their gardens and to farm the land as they had in Britain.

With the help of the Acclimatisation Societies enthusiastic individuals shipped to New Zealand the flora and fauna they were most familiar with. And so were brought out fruits and vegetables, decorative plants, shrubs and trees, assorted potential four-footed pests (as well as sheep and cattle) and an interesting range of birds — mostly British, but some from other parts of the old empire.

Faced with this onslaught, and the steady clearance of bushland, the majority of the indigenous species retreated, and diminished in numbers. But gradually things stabilised. Imported blackbirds moved happily into the bush. Tuis, silvereyes, grey warblers, fantails and others adapted to the New Zealand version of civilised living. So we now have quite a nicely mixed bag to study and record.

I am sometimes asked to identify 'a strange-looking bird' which has turned out to be merely a starling going through a change of plumage. It is also easy for the novice to confuse a yellowhammer with a canary. In this book I have illustrated some of the changes of plumage through the seasons and during the growth from nestling, to juvenile, to adult. In some species males and females vary considerably and these I have shown in pairs, while only one specimen is illustrated when the sexes are the same.

Although the paintings are the main reason for the book, I have tried to widen its value by incorporating something of each bird's family background and interesting overseas relatives.

the beginning

The birds seen in New Zealand could be categorised, somewhat arbitrarily, as follows:

Endemic	Found and breeding in New Zealand only.
Native or indigenous	Found and breeding in New Zealand, but also found in other countries.
Introduced	Released into New Zealand by man.
Self-introduced	Australian strays that have settled here.
Migratory	A two-way traffic; birds which breed here, e.g., gannets, cuckoos; and birds which breed in the northern hemisphere, e.g., godwits.

♂ male   ♀ female

Books used for reference

Collins Guide to the Birds of New Zealand, R. A. Falla *et al.*, 1985, Collins.

Annotated Checklist of the Birds of New Zealand, F. C. Kinsky *et al.*, 1970, A. H. & A. W. Reed.

The Reader's Digest Complete Book of New Zealand Birds, Reader's Digest, Sydney, 1985, Reed Methuen.

Taxonomic change. The scientific name of the spur-winged plover has been changed from *Lobibyx novaehollandiae* to *Vanellus miles*, but the earlier name has been retained in this book. (See pages 23-24.)

Family PHASIANIDAE:
Pheasants, Quails, Partridges

A worldwide family of ground dwelling birds which includes jungle fowl and peafowl. There is a great variety amongst these diverse species, from the small, cryptically coloured brown quail to the splendid elegance of the peacock. In many of the species, especially the pheasants, the males are brightly coloured while the females are usually dull and sombre. All are plump birds with strong legs on which they are rapidly mobile. Some species have, above and behind the toes, sharp spurs which are used in defence or aggression during the breeding season. All have small, rounded wings suitable for acceleration in time of danger. Although they have such a quick take-off they are unable to fly any distance. Their short, stubby bills are designed for seed eating and for searching amongst ground debris for food. At least seven species of game birds have been introduced into New Zealand, some unsuccessfully. Three of the more familiar are the pheasant, introduced during the 1840s and 1850s, the California quail, introduced from America about 1865, and the Australian brown quail during the 1860s.

Pheasant

Pheasant — *Phasianus colchicus*. 80 cm.

Since the so-called English *Phasianus colchicus* and the Chinese ring-necked *Phasianus torquatos* were released during the nineteenth century, interbreeding has taken place and now many of the birds are hybrids showing variations in colouring. They are found in scrub land around pasture and coastal areas of the North Island and eastern districts of the South Island. One cock will mate with up to ten females, but does not take part in the incubation of the eggs. Nests are lined hollows in thick cover. Seven to 15 olive-brown eggs are laid.

California quail — *Lophortyx californicus*. 25 cm.
Brown quail — *Synoicus ypsilophorus*. 18 cm.

These quails live in small coveys amongst scrub areas and pasture land. Their food consists of seeds, grasses, clover and insects. During the breeding season the coveys separate into pairs which take up their own

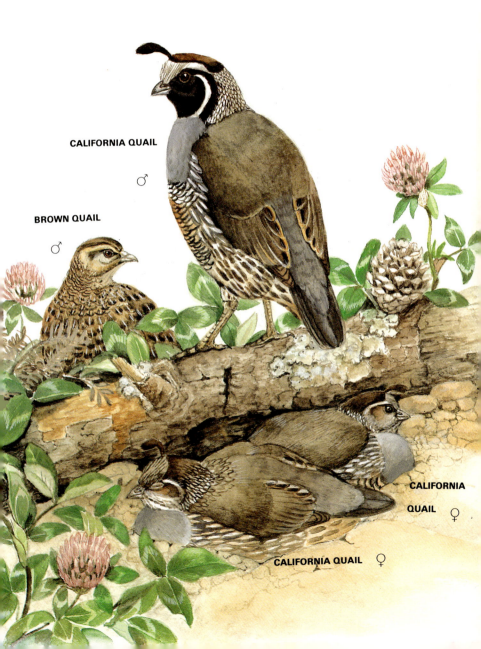

(Quails continued)

breeding territories. The nests are lined depressions on the ground in dense cover. The female California quail will lay about 14 creamy-white eggs spotted and streaked with brown, and the brown quail about 11 white eggs, freckled with olive-brown. The hens incubate while the males keep guard nearby. Both rear the chicks.

Pheasant chick.

Young Brown Quail

California Quail chick.

Family PLOCEIDAE: Sparrows, Weavers

The Ploceidae includes over 140 species of mainly seed eating birds. In this group are the whydahs, bishop birds, quelea and the weaver birds of Africa. They are mostly small birds with strong, cone-shaped bills designed for cracking seeds. They live in colonies and are the architects of intricately woven bottle-shaped nests.

The already widespread subfamily of sparrows was introduced into America, Australia and New Zealand. Thus through the agency of man the house sparrow is now one of the most familiar small birds.

Family PRUNELLIDAE:
Accentors, Hedge sparrow — *Prunella modularis*

Of the 13 species of accentors found throughout the world, the hedge sparrow is the only one to be introduced into New Zealand. They are secretive birds which spend a lot of time on the ground.

Sparrows showing aggression

Sparrows bathing

House sparrow —
Passer domesticus. 14.5 cm.

The only true sparrow to be introduced into New Zealand, this perky, bold, noisy bird is unique in the way it has adapted to a man-made environment and is at home in busy streets as well as gardens and pasture land. Unlike the related weaver birds, they are untidy nest builders, making bulky constructions in crevices, buildings and trees. Three to seven greyish-white eggs streaked with brown are laid, and one pair will raise up to four broods each year. Although mainly seed eaters, they will gladly scrounge any human leftovers or discards.

Family MUSCICAPIDAE: Flycatchers

Fantails are members of a worldwide family. They are insectivorous birds that usually take their prey in flight. Their bills are flat and short with bristles at the base. All build cup-shaped nests and lay spotted eggs. *Rhipidura* are found in Australia, New Zealand and the islands to the north as far as the Equator.

Family SYLVIIDAE: Warblers

A large complex family of insect eating birds found throughout Africa, Europe, Asia, Indonesia and the Pacific, with one or two species in North America. Opinions differ on the way some species are grouped.

Family CUCULIDAE: Cuckoos

A large, diversified family of birds found throughout the world, ranging in size from the small shining cuckoo (16 cm) to the large channel-billed cuckoo (61 cm). Characteristic of this family are their feet with two toes forward and two backwards. All tree cuckoos are parasitic and lay their eggs in the nests of other birds. Only two cuckoos breed in New Zealand — the shining cuckoo and the long-tailed cuckoo.

Fantail — *Rhipidura fuliginosa.* 16 cm.
Grey warbler — *Gerygone igata.* 11 cm.
Shining cuckoo — *Chalcites lucidus.* 16 cm.

Another bird that has adjusted well to human environments is the inquisitive, fearless fantail, even to the extent of entering houses in search of insects. Never still, they dart here and there in search of spiders, and insects which are mostly taken in flight.

Because of their sombre appearance, grey warblers are quite inconspicuous amongst the foliage of trees and shrubs, and are more often heard than seen. Their song is a clear, sweet warble.

The shining cuckoo migrates down from the Pacific Islands around September each year and remains in New Zealand for the breeding season. They are parasitic, mostly on grey warblers, using them as foster parents.

All these species are insectivorous.

Family ZOSTEROPIDAE: Silvereyes

A family of around 80 species of small, greenish-brown birds found in Africa, Asia, Australia and down through the South Pacific to New Zealand. They are relatively small birds with sharply pointed bills, and have brush-tipped tongues used for extracting nectar from flowers. They will perform amazing acrobatics to obtain food. In New Zealand they are known as silvereyes, but in other countries as white-eyes.

Silvereye — *Zosterops lateralis*. 12 cm.

The silvereyes were self-introduced from Australia during the 1800s and when first noticed by the Maori were named tauhou — stranger. Now common throughout the country, they move about in noisy, active flocks, feeding on fruit, nectar and insects found in shrubs, plants and trees. Because of their liking for aphids they were named blight-birds.

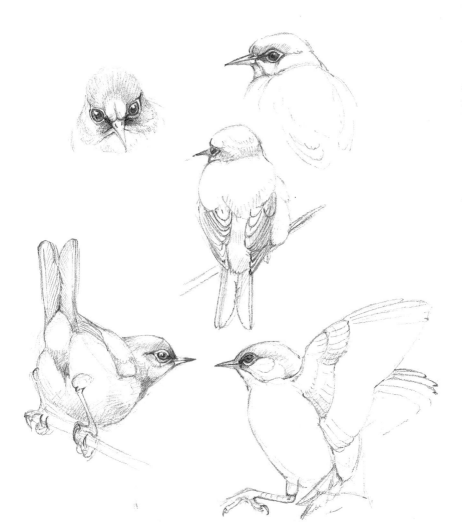

(Silvereyes continued)

Both male and female share in the building of their dainty, frail, cup-shaped nests made from fine roots, moss, grasses and hair, and usually suspended between twigs of shrubs and trees. Three or four greenish-blue eggs are laid and incubation is shared by both parents. When the young leave the nest the family stay together for two or three weeks.

Family MELIPHAGIDAE: Honeyeaters, including Tui

A large family of small to medium-sized birds found mainly around Australia and New Guinea. The main characteristic of this family is the long tongue with filaments on the tip for extracting nectar from flowers. Their feeding methods make them important pollinators (note dusting of pollen on forehead). Although some species of honeyeaters have adapted to a change in habitat away from forests and are common, Hawaiian species which were once prolific are now on the endangered list.

Tui — *Prosthemadera novaeseelandia*. 31 cm.

One of the biggest native birds that have adjusted to life away from the forest and now found also in city environments are the tuis. With more food-bearing plants being grown in gardens and parks they have now become regular visitors and make their presence known with their distinct musical song. They are usually seen in pairs and the males will aggressively defend territory, noisily chasing away any intruders. Although they seem to be clumsy birds, they will go through amazing contortions to obtain nectar, fruit and insects hidden in trees. They fly considerable distances, even to offshore islands.

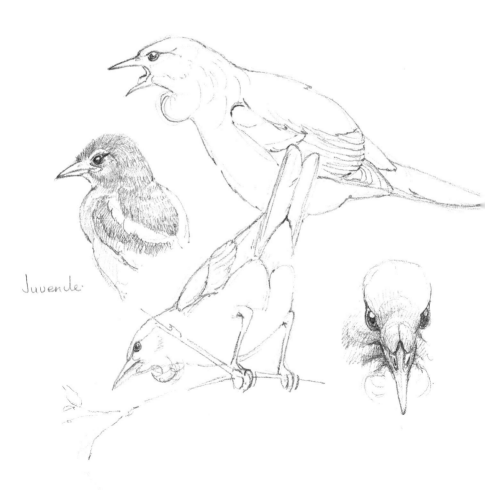

Juvenile.

Family RALLIDAE: Rails, Waterhens, Coots

Spread throughout the world, this family frequents swamps, wet places, lake edges and in some countries, forest areas. Rails and crakes have powerful legs and long toes that enable them to move over marshy ground with ease. Coots have lobed toes and spend most of their time on water. While the secretive rails and crakes have cryptic colouring, the pukeko and takahe have brilliant plumage. Most Rallidae are weak fliers.

Pukeko — *Phorphyrio melanotus*. 51 cm.

Groups of pukekos are common throughout the country and are often seen near cities, in the countryside and around lakes and swampy areas. They are large, ungainly looking birds with long legs and toes, but are able to move over water weeds with ease and can swim well. They are mainly vegetarian, but will feed on rhizomes, small fish and small birds

(Pukeko continued)

and animals. Food is sometimes held by a foot when feeding. Nests of grasses and rushes are built amongst vegetation on swampy ground and four to seven stone-coloured, blotchy eggs are laid. The chicks are able to leave the nest shortly after hatching.

Family CHARADRIIDAE: Plovers, Lapwings, Dotterels

A large family of 'wading' birds found throughout the world. Their habitat is usually the shoreline or open countryside near water, but some prefer semi-deserts. Of the 14 species which occur in New Zealand, some are very rare.

Family ARDEIDAE: Herons, Egrets, Bitterns

Mainly waterbirds, found throughout the world except in polar regions. They are large birds with broad wings, long necks, and long legs for wading through shallow water, grassland and marshes. A flying characteristic of this family is the slow wing beat and necks held in an 'S' position with heads close to their bodies.

CATTLE EGRET

SPUR-WINGED PLOVER

Spur-winged plover — *Lobibyx novaehollandiae*. 38 cm.
Cattle egret — *Bubulcus ibis*. 51 cm.

Both the elegant cattle egrets and the spur-winged plovers, recent immigrants from Australia, are now becoming well established throughout New Zealand. Flocks of cattle egrets are usually seen on pasture near water in the company of sheep and cattle, while the plovers prefer pasture with short cover or where crops have been growing. Plovers choose a nest site on the ground away from grazing animals, and a pair will usually remain together. Three or four dark green-brown, heavily blotched eggs are laid in the shallow, cup-shaped nest and both parents help with the incubation. Chicks leave the nest shortly after hatching. The cattle egret has not yet been found nesting in New Zealand.

Cattle Egret
Breeding Plumage.
Spur-winged Plover
Young Spur-winged Plover.

Family HIRUNDINIDAE: Swallows, Martins

Distributed throughout the world, most members of the family are similar, with slender bodies, pointed wings and tails usually forked. Their legs are short with small feet, and they have short, flattened bills with wide gapes. They are insectivorous and take food and sometimes water on the wing. Swallows and martins are superficially similar to swifts and wood-swallows which reach New Zealand only rarely.

Swallow in the wind

Chicks.

Welcome swallow — *Hirundo neoxena*. 15 cm.

Found in the south-west Pacific and Australia, these swallows introduced themselves into New Zealand during the 1950s. They are now well established in most areas, even the distant Chatham Islands. They spend most of the time on the wing, swooping and diving as they 'hawk' insects. They are usually seen in pairs or even groups of up to 30 or

more, especially in autumn and winter. All the time a constant twittering is maintained. Favourite nesting sites are on buildings, under bridges, wharves and even water culverts. Cup-shaped nests of mud pellets strengthened with grass are cemented to a solid background. Three to five white eggs speckled with brown are laid.

Family PSITTACIDAE: Parrots and Parakeets

Members of the parrot family are found throughout the tropics and the southern hemisphere. There are about 330 species. Among the 16 found in New Zealand are the endemic kea, kaka, red-fronted parakeet, yellow-fronted parakeet and the rare kakapo. Like all members of the family they have strong curved bills to dehusk seeds, to break open fruit, and to grip branches when moving through the trees. The legs are usually short, with two toes pointing forward and two backwards, enabling the birds to hold their food.

Eastern rosella — *Platycercus eximius*. 33 cm.

Eastern rosella — *Platycercus eximius.* 33 cm.

This colourful parakeet, accidentally introduced from its native Australia, has now established itself in many parts of the North Island, with a small colony near Dunedin in the south. It seems to prefer open country bordering on bush, and is gradually becoming a suburbanite. A ground-feeder which unfortunately likes the orchardists' fruit and nuts. Little is known of its breeding habits in New Zealand.

Family ALCEDINIDAE: Kingfishers

Only two species of this widespread family are found in New Zealand, the kookaburra which was introduced and the native New Zealand kingfisher. Kingfishers tend to be similar in shape and behaviour, even though there is a considerable difference in size between the 45 cm kookaburras and the 24 cm New Zealand kingfishers. They all have strong bills, large heads with short necks and legs. There are two groups of kingfishers, the fishing species which plunge into water for fish and the forest species which live on insects, lizards and worms and can be seen away from water. The New Zealand kingfishers belong to the latter group.

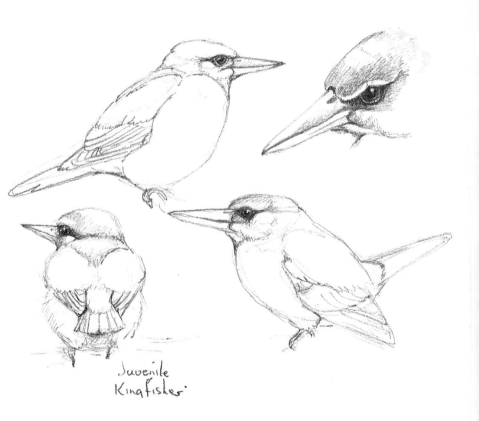

Juvenile Kingfisher

New Zealand kingfisher — *Halcyon sancta.* 24 cm.

Common throughout the country and often seen perched on overhead wires patiently watching for insects, small vertebrates and worms on the ground below. They will often beat their prey against a hard object before swallowing it. Kingfishers dig nest tunnels by repeatedly diving at a clay bank or rotten log until a hole is made. Four or five white eggs are laid on the bare earth or wood floor which soon becomes very polluted as they are untidy housekeepers. Both birds incubate and rear the young.

Family ACCIPITRIDAE:
Eagles, Hawks, Harriers, Kites

A large family of birds of prey found throughout the world. Varying in size from the 28 cm sparrowhawks to the large 90 cm wedge-tailed eagle, all are masters of soaring and gliding as they search for prey. Characteristic of these birds are strong hooked bills and powerful talons.

Family STRIGIDAE: Typical Owls

This worldwide family ranges in size from the tiny elf owl (6 cm) to the large (68 cm) eagle owls. They have large round eyes and bristles around their hooked bills. Their feet are very strong with sharp, hooked claws which enable them to carry prey to a perch.

HARRIER

LITTLE OWL

Harrier — *Circus approximans.* 60 cm.
Little owl — *Athene noctua.* 23 cm.

The harriers are handsome native birds of prey. Although their habitat is open country they can be observed near towns and cities. On their own or in pairs they glide on wind currents searching for the rabbits, mice, insects, frogs and lizards which make up their diet.

The introduced little owls differ from other nocturnal species of their family by often appearing during the day to hunt their prey of insects, lizards and frogs. They are quite common and widespread in the South Island and can be seen perched on fence posts and on the limbs of trees. Nests are built in holes in trees, buildings, earth banks and even in rabbit burrows. They lay three eggs which are incubated by the female.

Little Owl

Harrier chick

Family STURNIDAE: Starlings, Mynas

A large family of noisy, aggressive birds which spend a lot of time on the ground swaggering around, breaking into a hopping run when food is sighted. Although starlings are basically dark in colouring they have attractive iridescent plumage. Some of the African species have feathering of the most brilliant blues, purples, oranges and yellows. Able to live with man, starlings and mynas are well established around the world. Although many have a harsh and grating song, others are very musical and great mimics, imitating other birds, and when tame can learn to talk. Both species form large, noisy roosts.

Starling — *Sturnus vulgaris*. 20 cm.

After starlings were introduced from Europe into New Zealand in the 1860s they soon became well established and are now common throughout the country. They have a varied diet of insects, worms, grubs and fruit, and may be seen on mud flats searching for crabs. Nests of untidy heaps of grass lined with feathers are built in holes of trees and buildings. They will make use of a nest box. Four or five pale blue eggs are laid.

Starling — *Sturnus vulgaris*. 20 cm.

Myna — *Acridotheres tristis*. 24 cm.

Mynas were introduced into New Zealand from India in the 1870s, and are now well established in the North Island. The South Island is too cold for successful breeding and only the occasional bird is seen.

Myna — *Acridotheres tristis*. 24 cm. (continued)
They are smart, aggressive birds and have earned a bad reputation for attacking nests of other birds. Their diet consists of insects, worms, caterpillars, fruit, and they will spend time on the roadside picking up scraps of food and insects killed by cars. Like the starling they nest in holes and will make every effort to get into a nest box. A clutch of three to six blue eggs is laid and incubated by the female. Both parents rear the young.

Juvenile

Family TURDIDAE: Thrushes

A large family which is almost worldwide. Some are among the most renowned songbirds, including the nightingales, robins, hermit thrushes, wood thrushes, mistle thrushes, redwings, ring-ouzels and fieldfares, while the robins and bluebirds are known for their beauty. Closely related to the Old World species of warblers and flycatchers, they are mainly robust, ground birds of the countryside with strong wings. They eat worms, berries, fruit and insects, but do not take their prey on the wing like flycatchers.

Song thrush — *Turdus philomelos.* 23 cm.

Blackbird — *Turdus merula.* 25 cm.

Both are renowned for their song which is heard during winter and spring when territories are being set for the breeding season. Thrushes crack the shells of snails by hitting them on any hard object. The substantial cup-shaped nests of grasses, twigs and mosses bound together

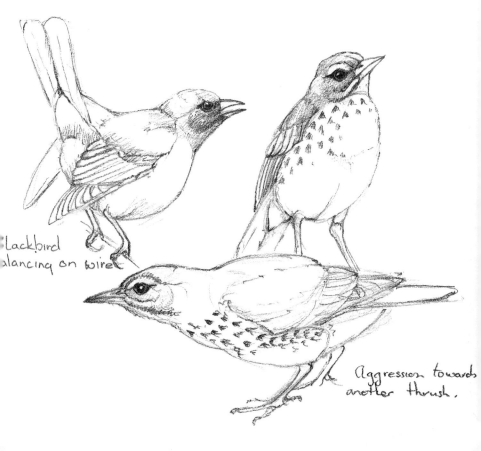

Blackbird balancing on wire

Aggression towards another thrush.

(Song thrush and blackbird continued)
with mud are similar, but the thrushes line theirs with a layer of rotten wood or mud mixed with saliva. The eggs of both species are bluish marked with dark spots or blotches.

(See page 35 for colour illustrations of juvenile song thrush and blackbird.)

Family EMBERIZIDAE: Buntings

Another complex family consisting of species of buntings, grosbeaks, the colourful tanagers and the honeyeaters of the tropics. Buntings are medium sized, seed eating birds which build their open, cup-shaped nests either close to or on the ground. In New Zealand there are two buntings, the yellowhammer, widespread throughout the country, and the cirl bunting which is common in the South Island, but rarely seen in the north.

Yellowhammer — *Emberiza citrinella*. 16 cm.

Cirl bunting — *Emberiza cirlus*. 16 cm.

Yellowhammers are seen in flocks in open countryside and sometimes in gardens near towns and cities. Cirl buntings feed in small flocks and are sometimes seen in the company of yellowhammers. Male yellowhammers are quite conspicuous when in flight while the male cirl buntings are less striking. Yellowhammers nest near or on the ground, but cirl buntings prefer a site higher in a shrub or bush. Their three or four pale eggs vary in colours between species but are all darkly streaked.

Family FRINGILLIDAE: Finches

These small to medium sized, seed eating birds are highly sociable and usually seen in groups as they move about the countryside. During their undulating flight they are constantly calling to each other with a pleasant, twittering song. All have strong, cone-shaped bills designed for breaking into seeds, berries and fruit. The females build the nests which are cup-shaped constructions of grasses, moss, spiders' webs and lined with soft materials. During the 1860s four species were introduced into New Zealand and are now widespread.

Chaffinch — *Fringilla coelebs*. 15 cm.

Attractive finches, quite at home in city parks, gardens, farmland and the outer areas of bush, where they are more often heard than seen. They move about in small flocks but individual birds can be seen feeding on fallen seeds, moving over the ground with short, quick steps which give them a bobbing action. After the females have built their nests they lay clutches of three to five greenish-blue eggs with dark blotches.

Greenfinch — *Carduelis chloris*. 15 cm.

Common in country areas, pine plantations and bush verges. Seeds form the larger part of their diet, and they will pull apart rose-hips, crab apples and cotoneaster berries to reach the seeds. During the winter they gather in flocks and will roost together at night. Although they use the same materials as the other finches, their nests are not quite so compact. Four or five bluish-white eggs with dark blotches are laid.

Redpoll — *Carduelis flammea*. 12 cm.

Redpolls are small, dainty finches found in various habitats throughout the country up to, and above, the bush line. Although seed eaters they will attack and damage the buds on fruit trees. The females build small, compact nests and lay three to six bluish-green, brown-blotched eggs.

Goldfinch — *Carduelis carduelis*. 12.5 cm.

The goldfinches with their bright plumage and sweet song are one of the most popular species found in gardens and the countryside. Cheerful flocks can be seen feeding on seeding plants, especially scotch thistles and lavender. The females build delicate nests and lay three to six bluish-white, blotched eggs.

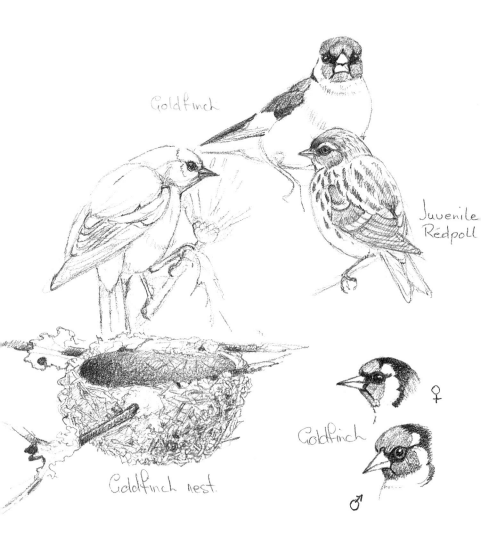

Family ALAUDIDAE: Larks

Skylarks are found in Africa, Europe and Asia and have been introduced to other countries around the world. They are medium sized birds of rather subdued colouring but are remarkable songsters. Mainly ground dwelling birds, they move about at a walk instead of hopping as they search for seeds and insects. The skylark has been an inspiration to many poets and musicians.

Family MOTACILLIDAE: Pipits, Wagtails

Pipits and wagtails are trim, slender birds that spend a lot of time on the ground, and like the skylark walk and run when searching for food. Their flight is undulating and pairs communicate with a loud call. Pipits are similar in appearance to skylarks but are only distantly related. Both have very long hind toes. Wagtails are almost entirely restricted to the Old World but pipits are nearly cosmopolitan.

Pipits

Juvenile Skylark.

Juvenile Pipit

Skylark — *Alauda arvensis*. 18 cm.

New Zealand Pipit — *Anthus novaeseelandiae*. 19 cm.

Skylarks, an introduced species, and the native pipit are both found in open country, tussock land and the roadside. Although similar in colouring and quite inconspicuous on the ground, there are slight differences. Skylarks have crests on their heads and pipits have longer tails which are 'flicked' as they move about. Both build well concealed nests on the ground in clumps of grass. During the breeding season male skylarks hover high above the ground pouring forth their delightful song.

SKYLARK

Family CRACTICIDAE: Magpies

A family of eight species of Australian birds (including currawongs and butcherbirds) with strong dagger-like bills. Found in pairs or in small groups, these fearless birds are highly territorial and will attack and chase any intruder. Their loud, melodious song is heard at its best early in the morning. Magpies have been kept as pet birds and are very good mimics.

Family CORVIDAE: Rook, Crows, Ravens

The only species of this family to be found in New Zealand are the introduced rooks which belong to a worldwide family of highly adaptable, sociable birds. They are large, aggressive and noisy. They are not popular in horticultural areas as they feed on crops and scrounge the food of domestic animals.

White-backed magpie — *Gymnorhina hypoleuca*. 42 cm.
Black-backed magpie — *Gymnorhina tibicen*. 40 cm.

These Australian birds were introduced into New Zealand during the 1860s and are found in many parts of the country. They are mainly insectivorous but will feed on invertebrates, other small creatures and occasionally grass and clover. Even though they are birds of the open spaces they can be seen in parks and well grassed areas. Females build bulky nests of twigs lined with soft materials high in tall trees such as pines or gum trees. Two to five bluish-green, darkly blotched eggs are laid. These can vary slightly in colouring.

Rook — *Corvus frugilegus*. 45 cm.

Since rooks were released in New Zealand in the 1860s the main rookeries are still in Hawke's Bay and in Canterbury. During the breeding season they gather in flocks and build their untidy nests in large colonies in tall trees. Three or four pale blue or green, brown-blotched eggs are laid. Rooks have conspicuous bare skin around the base of the bill.